SHELTERING THOUGHTS
ABOUT LOSS AND GRIEF

BY SHARON GILCHREST O'NEILL

TATE PUBLISHING, LLC

IN MEMORY OF LIVIA

My Mother
My Friend
My Child
My Angel
My Eternal Wings

WITH APPRECIATION

In the late 1970s, I was very fortunate
to become part of a committed, creative,
and caring group of professionals
who founded the first freestanding hospice
in the United States,
The Connecticut Hospice, Inc.

I am forever grateful to have been part of such
an inspiring and significant initiative.
Sheltering Thoughts,
no doubt, emerged from this experience.

FOREWORD

The death of someone we love brings about tremendous mental, emotional, and physical stress. Numbness gives way to immobilizing pain and confusion. Coping skills fail and comforting routine may blur or disappear. We wonder what is the right way to grieve? We seek a timetable for grieving, and we ask when the pain will ease. We sense life, as we knew it, is forever changed, but wonder what our changed life will be. While there are fellow travelers on the grief journey, the particular path we follow is uniquely our own. We move, fall back, struggle, and progress in our individual times and ways.

In *Sheltering Thoughts*, the author shares her own insights and the wisdom of many ages and cultures in the quotations she has chosen. Readers are invited to select whatever speaks most meaningfully to their own experiences. As you move from the moment of death through the days, weeks, and months of living in a world without the physical presence of your beloved, we wish for you healing and peace.

The Bereavement Team, Connecticut Hospice

SHELTERING THOUGHTS . . .

To comfort you in your loss . . .
To give you strength and courage

To
Find your own way to grieve,
To shed the tears and sadness in your
Heart,

And to always remember.

Memories . . .

THIS BOOK IS DEDICATED
to the memory of:

_____

from:

_____

The death of a friend, a loved one,
a family member,
and even an acquaintance,
can touch us in ways that we never expect,
never anticipate.
We find ourselves struggling . . .
to make sense, to understand . . .
the death itself and our reactions to it.

Death, for most of us,
presents great challenges in our
thinking about our meanings of life,
most broadly,
and about our own lives on this earth
and their purposes.

There are few experiences in life
that affect us like death.

DEATH IS
OVERWHELMING,

and with a power
that can produce growth within us
like we have not known before.
Death leads us beyond our mind,
our intellect, our reasoning,

Beyond our physical body . . .

Because death reaches right into our hearts
and the deepest places in our souls,
into our spirits,
into the very core of our beings,
and it takes a good, firm hold.

Allow yourself to be held,
to feel death in your heart and in your soul,
for in this time lies waiting
a most profound opportunity.

You always have two ways to run.
Away from . . . or towards . . .

Joe Gores

Given a choice between grief and nothing
I'd choose grief.

William Faulkner

If we can live with the knowledge
that death is our constant companion,
traveling on our "left shoulder,"
then death can become in the words of Don Juan,
our "ally," still fearsome
but continually a source of wise counsel.

M. Scott Peck, M.D.

DEATH IS DISORIENTING.

It is a feeling . . .
out of body, out of mind, out of place, out of time.

Death slows us down.
It *is* a time to be in slow motion.
It *is* a time to pause more often, to stop more often.

Do be quiet. Do be still.
Most of us are too active, too purposeful, too verbal . . .
too much of our days.

Slowing down
allows us to look around in new or forgotten ways
that we normally do not allow ourselves the time for.

When did you last look up at a star?
Allow someone just to hold your hand?
Spend a few hours without a plan,
without a purpose, without being productive?

WHAT WOULD FEEL GOOD FOR YOU RIGHT NOW ?

Grief is universal.
At the same time it
is extremely personal.
Heal in your own way.

Earl A. Grollman

Sorrows cannot all be explained away
in a life truly lived,
grief and loss accumulate like possessions.

Stephan Kanfer

TREASURED . . .

POSSESSIONS

DEATH IS A TIME TO REVISIT OUR SENSES.

Most of us are exposed to
such constant and competing stimuli
that our senses are overworked and too often numb
to the pleasures surrounding us.

So rest your senses from the typical, daily stimuli.
Take time instead to consider things
that more recently have not gotten your attention . . .

The feel of a cool breeze across your face,
the view from a usually unnoticed window,
the sounds of a child,
the taste of a special tea,
the smell of the woods.

As the days go by, allow them in.

Turn your face to the sun
and the shadows fall behind you.

Maori Proverb

Preservation of the soul means refusing
to relinquish the body and its sensual
appreciation of texture, color, multiplicity,
pain, and joy.

David Whyte

DEATH CAN HELP US TO BE MORE CONSCIOUS

in ways that have been lost to us lately.

What catches your eye?
Hold your gaze and consider what is before you
for more than the quick, passing moment.

Reconsider your field of vision at times.
Enlarge it; restrict it. Look up and out, for example,
when you open the front door to take in the mail.

Close your eyes from time to time
and focus on another sense.

LISTEN TO MUSIC . . .

Music is a wonder that truly enhances our lives.
It has the power to bring our feelings to the surface.
Listen longer than usual
and without doing another thing.

Music is the medicine of the breaking heart.

Leigh Hunt

There is nothing better than music
as a means for the upliftment of the soul.

Hazrat Inayat Khan

NATURE . . .

It is restorative.
Its elements nurture us . . .
our bodies and our souls.
Nature helps us to grow.

TAKE WALKS.

Feel the warmth of the sunlight,
the gentle sensation of rain drops . . .
Take in the smells of the garden,
the taste of the salt air sprays.

Nature enlivens all of our senses
and reminds us what it feels like to be alive,
what it means to be fully human.
It clears our heads
and helps us to open up and listen to our hearts.

We come to know ourselves better in nature.

DEATH IS A TIME FOR NEW PERSPECTIVE TAKING,

a time for contemplation . . .
a time to nurture our creativity.

Reexamine, reevaluate, and pose questions
about your life.

WHAT IS IMPORTANT TO YOU?

What were your dreams, and why
did you let them go?

What has been lost along the way
of living your life?

Recapture it.

As Plato long ago suggested so succinctly,
"the unexamined life is not worth living."

I have never done the thing that I wanted to
in all my life.

Sinclair Lewis (Babbitt)

Nothing can bring you peace but yourself.

Ralph Waldo Emerson

Without the awareness of death, one would be only an ordinary man involved in ordinary acts. One would lack the necessary potency, the necessary concentration that transforms one's ordinary time on earth into magical power.

Carlos Castaneda

SEE THE WORLD
ANEW . . .

Allow yourself to imagine, to dream,
to think in different ways.
Take in new knowledge, new ideas,
new experiences . . .
They are nourishment.

Challenge yourself
to examine your thought patterns,
your habits, your rituals.

Change happens first in our imaginations.
We must be as creative as we possibly can;
we must go beyond
how we have known the world.

DEATH
STIRS THINGS UP.

It challenges and it disrupts.
It is confusing and chaotic.
However, if you remain in the chaos . . .
if you tolerate the chaos . . .
something new will be revealed to you.

Scientists have learned
that within the randomness of chaos
there is more sense than we know;
there are patterns of exquisite beauty
and tremendous wonderment.

THE CHAOS WILL
BRING FORTH A CLARITY
AND A VIVIDNESS,

if we are able to ride it out.
We become more attuned, more attentive to the world.

You will surprise yourself.
You will make discoveries.
You will come to know new pieces of yourself.
You will have new perspectives, new priorities . . .
You will delight
in putting yourself back together differently.
Having stayed with the chaos,
you will be rewarded with a newfound wisdom.

It is by going down into the abyss
that we recover the treasures of life.

Joseph Campbell

The demon that you can swallow gives you its power,
and the greater life's pain, the greater life's reply.

Joseph Campbell

Truly, it is in darkness that one finds the light,
so when we are in sorrow,
then this light is nearest of all to us.

Meister Eckhart

The world is round
and the place which may seem like the end
may also be only the beginning.

Ivy Baker Priest

Be aware of your energy.

HOW DO YOU USE YOUR ENERGY ?

WHERE DO YOU SEE IT DISPERSED ?

Maybe it is time to redirect some portion
of your energy.

The ocean has her ebbings ~ so has grief.

Thomas Campbell

There is a great deal of pain in life and perhaps the only pain that can be avoided is the pain that comes from trying to avoid pain.

R.D. Laing

Survival, I know, is to begin again.

Judy Collins

OUR CULTURE PREFERS TO DENY, TO REPRESS DEATH,

to keep it compartmentalized from the rest of life.
We feel we should experience death as a separate entity
for some period of time,
and then go on with life.
But life and death are so intimately connected.
To separate death from life
does not allow death to touch us, to teach us,
to work its wonders upon us,
to ultimately stimulate our learning and our growth
about life and living.

While grief is fresh,
every attempt to divert it only irritates.

Samuel Johnson

Concealed grief has no remedy.

Turkish Proverb

Give sorrow words; the grief that
does not speak
Whispers the o'er-fraught heart
and bids it break.

Macbeth, Act IV, sc.3

Shrinking away from death is something
unhealthy and abnormal
which robs the second half of life
of its purpose.

C.G. Jung

All sorrows can be borne
if you put them into a story
or tell a story about them.

Isak Dinesen

For life and death are one,
even as the river and the sea are one.

Kahlil Gibran

ONLY BY EMBRACING DEATH

AND INCORPORATING IT
INTO OUR LIVES

ARE WE ABLE TO EXPAND
OURSELVES, ENLARGE OUR
LIVES . . .

THUS MAKING WAY FOR THE
NEW AND WONDERFUL.

We are healed from suffering
only by experiencing it to the full.

Marcel Proust

Sorrow is like a cloud;
when it becomes heavy it falls.

Native American Proverb

By embracing the feelings
that come at times of ending,
as well as the thoughts and feelings
that linger for a very long time afterwards
we become renewed persons.

Thomas Moore

THIS **IS** A TIME TO THINK ABOUT DEATH,

to consider its meaning . . .
what you hold in your head
and what you hold in your heart.

Death is a time that helps you get closer
to your beliefs,
to God, to your religion, to certain worldviews,
to faith.

Do not worry that you cannot seem to
understand death . . .
that you cannot seem to make sense of things.

But life has taught me that it knows better plans than we can imagine, so that I try to submerge my own desires, apt to be too insistent, into a calm willingness to accept what comes, and to make the most of it, then wait again.

I have discovered that there is a Pattern, larger and more beautiful than our short vision can weave.

Julia Seton

A worldly loss often turns into spiritual gain.

Hazrat Inayat Khan

When you are deluded and full of doubt,
even a thousand books of scripture
are not enough.
When you have realized understanding,
even one word is too much.

Fen-Yang

The story is told that one of the elders lay dying in Scete, and the brethren surrounded his bed, dressed him in the shroud and began to weep. But the elder opened his eyes and laughed. He laughed another time, and then a third time. When the brethren saw this, they asked him, saying: "Tell us, Father, why are you laughing while we weep?" He said to them: "I laughed the first time because you fear death. I laughed the second time because you are not ready for death. And the third time I laughed because from labors I go to my rest." As soon as he had said this, he closed his eyes and died.

Desert Hermit Zen

DEATH, CONCEIVED OF
IN THE CONTEXT OF
THIS UNIVERSE,

BY OUR MORTAL BODIES,
IS AN IMPOSSIBLE TASK.

The great thinkers,
like Einstein and Michelangelo,
considered death a wonderful mystery
to contemplate in our world,
but a mystery to understand and behold
in another dimension.

Every exit is an entry somewhere else.

Tom Stoppard

Death ~ the last voyage, the longest, the best.

Thomas Wolfe

I shall hear in Heaven.

Beethoven

AND WHAT OF THAT OTHER DIMENSION?

A place where growth continues,
a place where a part of us is indestructible . . .

Ponder; pursue your personal thoughts,
not for a finality of answers,
but in the spirit of a lifelong learning,
relearning, refining process.

When we think we have final answers,
better understanding will always cease.

What had to be seen was that the Chris I missed so badly was not an object but a pattern, and that although the pattern included the flesh and blood of Chris, that was not all there was to it. The pattern was larger than Chris and myself, and related us in ways that neither of us understood completely and neither of us was in complete control of.

Robert M. Pirsig

There is no death, only a change of worlds.

Dr. Robert Anthony

My love came back to me
Under the November tree
Shelterless and dim.
He put his hand upon my shoulder,
He did not think me strange or older,
Nor I, him.

Frances Cornford

CONTEMPLATE DEATH AND GRIEVE TO YOUR FULLEST.

You will then be most alive.

Even a happy life
cannot be without a measure of darkness
and the word 'happiness'
would lose its meaning
if it were not balanced by sadness.

C.G. Jung

.
.
.

Happiness . . .

Sadness . . .

I lost both my parents to death ~
first my father and then my mother ~
while I was still a boy.
That was a colossal storm, an irreversible wind
that changed my destiny.
I didn't command that wind
and I couldn't make it give back
what it had taken away.
But it was my wind and I had to sail it
until it led me at last to a sheltered cove.

Richard Bode

There is no coming to consciousness
without pain.

C. G. Jung

After a great pain
a formal healing comes.

Emily Dickinson

DEATH HELPS US REDEFINE OUR VALUES.

Our culture stresses acquisitions
and the joy of accumulation.
We continually learn how to add to our
possessions,
but rarely how to take away from our
possessions
or how to deal with imposed loss,
except by keeping busy or replacing the loss.

We are never prepared for loss.

LETTING GO OF SOME THINGS CAN BE EXHILARATING.

It makes room in our hearts and in our souls for new things that will come if there is space.

DEATH CAN HELP US . . .

come to know better
the abundance in our lives
and what it is that we truly appreciate.
The desire to acquire
takes on different dimensions.

Those things that hurt, instruct.

Benjamin Franklin

Most of life's luxuries,
and many of the so-called comforts of life,
are not only not indispensable,
but positive hindrances
to the elevation of mankind.

Henry David Thoreau

When one door of happiness closes,
another opens;
but often we look so long at the closed door
that we do not see the one which has been
opened for us.

Helen Keller

Be vulnerable and receptive,
be courageous, and be patient.
Above all, look into your life to find ways
of sharing your love more deeply
with others now.

Sogyal Rinpoche

S HARE . . .

S HARE . . .

Self-pity in its early stages is as snug as a
feather mattress.
Only when it hardens does it become
uncomfortable.

Maya Angelou

DEATH IS EXHAUSTING.

It is enraging.
It is overwhelming.
It is disorienting.

IT SPINS YOU 'ROUND
AND 'ROUND.

Death is a struggle.
It is sad.
It is lonely.
It is depressing.
It is painful.
It fills us with anger and guilt,
Yet it holds forth a balance over time,
In what is lost and what is gained . . .

If we can be receptive and open,
And take in and learn
Like children again.

Sorrow makes us all children again.

Ralph Waldo Emerson

Learn to get in touch with silence
within yourself and know that everything
in this life has a purpose.
There are no mistakes, no coincidences,
all events are blessings
given to us to learn from.

Elisabeth Kubler~Ross

DO LEARN . . .

The general outlook is not that
the person has died,
but that the person has lived.

William Buchanan

DO LIVE . . .

Nothing must be postponed;
find eternity in each moment.

Henry David Thoreau

THIS IS A TIME TO REMEMBER.

NEVER ASK YOURSELF TO FORGET.

Our time with one who has died is always with us.
There is a quality, an essence
to their being that will go on forever . . .
It *is* everlasting.

Remember what the person has given you,
what you have learned from him,
through his life as well as in his death.

Remember his spirit.

Allow his words to guide you still,
his unique self to influence you still.

WHAT WILL YOU REMEMBER ?

One must discriminate between the mortal aspect
and the immortal aspect of one's own existence.
In the experience of my mother and father
who are gone,
of whom I was born,
I have come to understand that there is more
than what was our temporal relationship.

Joseph Campbell

The only truly dead
are those who have been forgotten.

Jewish Proverb

Her physical presence was no longer with us,
but I would not let her leave me.
I would see to it that she accompanied me
all the days of my life.

Sherwin B. Nuland

HOW WILL YOU REMEMBER ?

Love, like the ocean,
is vast and forever,
And sorrow, but a shadow
that moves over the sea.

John Gray

.
.
.
Forever . . .

WE CAN COMMUNICATE
IN A CHANGED WAY.

WE CAN CONTINUE THE
RELATIONSHIP
IN ANOTHER CONTEXT.

THIS PERSON CAN
REMAIN A PART OF US,
ALWAYS.

AND IN THIS WAY, WE
TRULY HONOR HER.

Death doesn't erase a relationship,
it simply places it in a different context.
Fostering our relationships to the dead
gives the soul its nourishment
of eternity, melancholy, mystery,
and the kind of relatedness
that is not literally of this world.

Thomas Moore

People come and go in life,
but they never leave your dreams.
Once they're in your subconscious,
they are immortal.

Patricia Hampl

Failure to mourn makes light of loss,
and undervalues the one lost.
And unmourned death is made meaningless.
Meaninglessness causes despair
and despair kills the soul.

Germaine Greer

And ever has it been that love knows
not of its own depth
until the hour of separation.

Kahlil Gibran

:
:

LOVE LOVE LOVE
LOVE LOVE . . .

All is never said.

Native American Proverb

In the beginning everything was in
relationship,
and in the end everything will be in
relationship again.
In the meantime, we live by hope.

Jean Lanier

H OPE . . .

THIS IS A TIME FOR OLD MEMORIES.

Get out the pictures, the letters,
the special gifts.
Watch the movies you shared;
visit the places where you ventured together.

Know that you will never forget this person.

We have unusual powers,
through our senses, to recall the past.
A smell, a vision, a sound, a taste, a touch . . .
do not be afraid to let them in.

Over time the memories from such recall
will be filled with comfort and peace.

But true love is a durable fire,
In the mind ever burning,
Never sick, never old, never dead,
From itself never turning.

Sir Walter Raleigh

... Life is eternal
And love is immortal
And death is only a horizon

Life is eternal
As we move into the light
And a horizon is nothing
Save the limit of our sight

Carly Simon

ETERNAL LOVE . . .

ABOUT THE AUTHOR

Sharon Gilchrest O'Neill, ED.S.,
is a Marriage & Family Therapist and Family
Business Consultant. She has worked for over
twenty-five years, both in private practice and
in the corporate setting, helping her clients to
examine assumptions, think creatively, and build
upon strengths. Sharon has been a graduate
instructor/advisor, a hospice volunteer, a NYC
Marathon finisher, and is the author of *Lur'ning,*
147 Inspiring Thoughts for Learning on the Job.
She lives in the woods of northern Westchester
County, New York, with her husband, Dennis,
and her son, Matthew.

Sharon can be contacted at
sheltering@optonline.net

Contact Sharon O'Neill at

sheltering@optonline.net
or order more copies of this book at

TATE PUBLISHING, LLC

127 East Trade Center Terrace
Mustang, Oklahoma 73064

(888) 361 - 9473

Tate Publishing, LLC

www.tatepublishing.com